They Are All Me

Copyright © 2015 Swimming with Elephants Publications
First Edition

All rights reserved. No portion of this publication may be reproduced, stored in a retrieval system, or transmitted in any form or by any other means, electronic, mechanical, photocopying, or recording without prior permission of Dominique Christina unless such copying is expressly permitted by federal copyright law. Address inquiries in permissions to:
Swimming with Elephants
Publications.swimmingwithelephants@gmail.com

Cover Art Copyright © 2015 Joshua Mays

They Are All Me

a collection of poetry

Dominique Christina

Table of Contents

Introduction 7

Summer of Violence 15
No Vowels, and No Consonants Either 19
Wolf Pack 21
Mothers of Murdered Sons 24
A Letter to Obama, Which Means Nothing 29
Karma 34
Birmingham Sunday 38
Because Kojo Went to War 43
A Poem for Coretta 48
Black Mass 52
Midnight Bridge 54
A Requiem for Renisha 56
Oh America… 58
Bodies are Only Bodies 61
The Sons of Oil Men 64
On the Subject of Eve 67
Gladiator Sorcery 69
Improbable Bird 71
Haiti, My Heart 73

Send an SOS to the President 75
Chain Gang 79
For Margaret Garner (28 days free until) 85
Strange Fruit 88
The Road That Was a Wolf 93
A Choir of Blackbirds 97
A Child Soldier Speaks… 99
September 2001 102
This is Before… 106
Bad Blood 108
The Period Poem 112
Katrina 117
Carry Your Books With You. 120

About the Author 122

Introduction

On a propitious December 21, 2014 I found myself checked into the Chinese Hospital of San Francisco with Chronic Obstructive Pulmonary Disease, or COPD. I'd been in that hospital in March of that year after my immune system apparently broke down into a pneumonia after the death of my closest friend for a generation, the editor and publisher of Left Curve magazine, Csaba Polony, with whom I worked for 33 years and who'd died earlier that month of stomach cancer. Fearing in December that the pneumonia had returned, I checked myself into the hospital.

As it turned out COPD was not as serious and I was able even to write while I was in hospital, and to make the remarkable discovery that's led to the publication of this book. Let me say first off that I don't usually watch television. I'd rather write or translate from other languages, or paint. I did write a bit at the Chinese Hospital, but I also indulged my fingers on a teevee remote----which on occasion are reserved only for watching either a baseball game or a boxing match--- and found to my surprise and delight a Channel 27, called Link, on which I viewed an anti-capitalist and anti-corporate-state talk by Chris Hedges.

Wow, thought I, a genuine progressive teevee channel for the People!

The following program introduced a poet I had never heard of, or read, Dominique Christina, intoning her poem, "Karma." From that very reading of hers, I knew I had experienced one of the very great poets of this land and I made up my mind that as soon as I recovered from my bout with COPD I was going to learn more of, and even make contact with, this African-American poet who had so moved me.

This I did a week later when, googling her name, I learned that she apparently had been the Women's Slam Champion in 2012, and again in 2014. This surprised me because, when she was reading "Karma" I saw PAGE, I saw BOOK----which is not usually the case when it comes to a lot of so-called Slam or spoken-word poetry I've heard. Usually a poet in that kind of competition is inspired by the muse of microphone, which feeds the subjectivity of the poet with the intensity of Delivery, which becomes the all-important entity.

This isn't the case with Dominique Christina. She has refused, completely refused to flee, finesse or fandango the brutal history of the African-American people, which is the story of the treacherous, murderous capitalist system itself----its revolution that wasn't a revolution in fact but an enslavement upon which the lie of "democracy" was built from the beginning and loaded like bricks on the backs of Black men and women.

So this is, first of all, a book of the rage of a people at the heart of what it means to be an American *of whatever color or stripe*. It's a rage that reveals the truth of a tyranny and oppression that's more than the tyranny over one segment of the population; it's a rage that is recognized by anyone who is a human being in a contemporary moment of human existence.

That is the greatness of this book: it's a rage whose authenticity's rooted in historical fact, with a lyrical righteousness of feeling and evocation that is undeniably poetic.

Yes, I speak of a poetry of rage at the heart of what it means to be a true poet in this land, which has assumed imperialist leadership in a technological war whose total mobilization of people-as-soldiers has left no one at peace. Rage against such tyranny is the most naturally passionate form of resistance. I've known this since the American war in Vietnam in 1965, i.e., that rage is the most authentic path to the expression of love in our language, just as Dominque Christina has probably known this for most of her life as an African-American woman and mother (See her biographical notes at the end of the texts).

The most widespread internationalization of poetry in the past 38 years has been the poetry of the HipHop/Rap generation which, since in its founding in The Bronx in 1977 (I was born and raised on Amadou Diallo Street, formerly Wheeler Avenue, in The Bronx), has migrated the world over and, with the birth of Slam poetry and Marc Smith's installation in 1986 to democratize poet and audience, an exciting dimension of spoken-word poetry has literally raised a generation of younger poets whose works are published, as I've suggested, "in the journal between the ears."

That is, because HipHop/Rap and Slam poetry were created not book-first but performance-first, and no doubt because the former began with African/Chicano-Americans, and the latter with a Chicagoan close to poets in the

Communist Labor Party, there has always been a political separation between the spoken-word---as though its poets didn't write their works!---and the written-word "literary" poets.

Until now. With *They Are All Me* Dominique Christina collapses that separation. Here is a book of depths of compassion along with her rage; of a linguistic brilliance and of praise for the entourage of African-American heroes and martyrs who are part of all our souls' memories.

She is an activist poet and teacher who answers the call---especially in these days of widely acknowledged police brutality---to be present in different cities, though she is a mother of four and lives in Denver, Colorado. After a recent trip to Baltimore following the protests against the murder of Freddie Gray, she wrote:

"I'm sort of shell-shocked from my time in Baltimore during the unrest. First thing you see is the National Guard holding huge automatic assault rifles in the middle of the city and instantly you know you're not in Kansas anymore. Then police and the military and tanks, rolling down the streets, and sitting idle next to parks and museums with men in uniform on top jeering at you and looking at you like you are the imposition and not them. Baltimore was a spectacle of horror long before Freddie Gray died but it holds an unspeakable hopelessness now. Row after row, block after block of boarded up homes, trash everywhere, no playgrounds, the schools are filthy, their doors boarded shut, no produce in the grocery stores, no money in the ATM machines. It's helter-skelter and it's all happening in an American city and there are kids everywhere and none of them look clean; all of them were hungry...every single one I met...hungry. But stoic and resolute. I never saw any victims in Baltimore. The only thugs I saw

were police officers. I was personally chased by riot police who pepper-sprayed me and the students I had with me for defying the curfew by one minute. They pointed their M16's at us. We were sprinting down dark streets in the Sandtown-Winchester neighborhood of Baltimore where Freddie Gray lived trying not to be captured. I/we ducked into the projects while many many people behind us were hit with billy clubs and pulled down by police officers who then kicked them and tossed them into a van. I saw them clothesline a girl who looked to be about 13. (That's a wrestling move) She hit her head hard on the concrete. Two women heard us, came out, and let us come inside their home until much of the noise and chaos subsided but we still went through hell getting back to our hotel rooms. I can't stop thinking about the people there. The five year-old I played basketball with while men with assault rifles were all around. How he couldn't go to school because it had been closed down. How 80% of the children in that community rely on the breakfast and lunch provided to them at school and so when they closed the school they effectively starved the children. I can't stop thinking about the 11 year-old in the gas mask I walked with in the middle of the street in defiance of a militarized police state and how he was sooooo much braver than I. How he had been starved and brutalized so long, there was nothing he wouldn't do to escape the degradation.

 And I think about my own privilege and how I have never been so acutely aware of it in my life. See, I got to leave...look how lucky I am. I got to leave hell...while so many others are burning."

I'm honored to be able to introduce this superb poet whose work graces us all with a strength and resonance that is a truly rare and yet a recognizable affirmation of the highest order.

----Jack Hirschman
San Francisco, 2015

They Are All Me

Summer of Violence

You'll ride through these neighborhoods.
You, the respectable taxpayer whizzing by the ruins
in your convenient cars,
avoiding the faces of children who cannot keep their skin.
The ones whose fingernails are not clean,
who pick the chicken bones bare and spit on sidewalks,
the unearned saunter of summer.
They're everywhere and nowhere and you'll say:
There's no crisis here,
and scuttle off to work
grateful for 401k's, department store slacks, and
wine-laced, one-night stands that
don't cost you anything to be so fucking free.

And I'll say:
Did you notice the ones who are gone?
Did you see the unpopulated stoops and alleyways?
The caterwauling yawp of
long ago black boy bodies who shut up their flesh
brick by bullet by blade?
Do you know there was a dirge
that hitched the city's steps to a limp?
How the corner boys knew they would die that summer.

It was 1993.
I buried four friends and the bodies kept coming
into Pipkin Mortuary.
I saw fourteen-year old boys pay for their funerals in advance
so their mamas would not hafta leave 'em at the city morgue

or borrow money from an auntie they never spoke to.
How they traded in their gold chains,
the paraphernalia of the oppressed,
for discount caskets and pre-printed obituaries.

How Tyree paid for his funeral
because he knew he would die in June.
How Marcus paid in advance for his interment
because he knew he would die in July.
How James and Richard brought in mason jars
filled with scrunched dollar bills because
they KNEW they would die in August.

Do you know ALL of them were right?
I sat at the wakes of boys who were not old enough
to drive a car or fall in love.

Do you know
all their mamas look the same on Sunday morning?
The polyester skirts, the pleated blouses,
their hair just curled, the same sizzle at the ears.
How I sang with the choirs that were heavy
with big black women born to slip grief around their necks
and cry Hosanna.

A practiced familiar hurt.

The media called it The Summer of Violence.
A blistering three months
where we were sooooo stingy with our suffering.
The fuckin' fecundity of negro boys
who were, nevertheless, good at dying.

Do you know
that Paul was shot in his chest on the way to school?
He was my favorite student.
I gave him chocolate bars and composition notebooks.
The only lie I ever told him was that he would survive.

Do you know
the machine that whirred and bleeped on his behalf
didn't announce the moment when his lungs,
peppered with 22 caliber bullets,
decided they were no longer interested in the dance of survival.
I didn't attend that funeral,
sent flowers to his grandmother instead,
tucked my sons into me,
became a wolf, where a woman should be,
woke up the next day and asked
the bloody-knuckle citizenry of black boys
to sit up straight in class, turn in their homework anyway.

The boys I know have no allegiance to their bodies,
with their necks jutting into midnight.
The boys whose subjects and verbs don't agree with each other.
These boys with their hypothetical futures
don't BELIEVE in your kind of tomorrow.

Your tomorrow has a bullet in it.
Ask Trayvon Martin.
Your tomorrow has a bullet in it.
Ask Jordan Davis.
Your tomorrow has a bullet in it.
Ask Michael Brown.

See, what you don't know is:
We're still trying to be here.
To give up an antebellum inheritance and
reach for the sound of
our own unBROKEN flesh.

Though we bleed best.
We're still trying to be here.
To throw roses into the abyss and say,
finally say,

"Here's my thanks to the monster
who didn't succeed in swallowing me alive."

No Vowels, and No Consonants Either

Ronnie did three years in
solitary confinement
but not for the murders,
just the drugs and the
way he sold 'em.

Woke up one morning
and couldn't remember his
daughter's name.
Other things.
Simple words like Love,
like Goodbye.

Language is slippery
when you don't use it,
when nobody speaks to you,
when no letters come.
Language is a graveyard
of carrier pigeons.
The rotting meat of
unsaid things
that made him curse God
harder than he did
when they killed his
uncle in front of him
when we were nine years old.

So he kept his head
in the lion's mouth,
gave his bones back to the dark

like so many boys he
pushed off the planet
trying to prove that the cosmic fight
of manhood is a dark altar
held up by the bones of
whoever's weakest.

It's funny:
> when I knew him he held doors open and
> loved his mama though she
> chain-smoked Marlboros and
> never paid the light bill,
> kept his shoes clean and
> his shirts tucked in.

The boy who became a man,
the one who learned the death-rattle
religion of solitary cells,
the bruised clergy of convicted men,

the one who forgot the sound of his voice,
who learned to hurt soundlessly,
damned to scratch for consonants
and vowels
roaring his spite in total silence---

The widest wound I know.

Wolf Pack

This is no lamentation.
No sorrow-filled woes.
This is for the fallen.
The ones struck down too soon.
For the would-have-been ones and
the could-have-been ones.
For the bodies that felt the full
audacity of helplessness.
For the limbs that were stretched by
the meanness of steel.

This is for Amadou Diallo
shot at 41 times as he reached for
his wallet in the vestibule of
his tenement and
Edward Anderson shot while cuffed and
on the ground and
Anthony Baez choked to death and
Frankie Arzuega shot in the back
and Rene Campos who was forced to
swallow more than half his t-shirt and
Garland Carter shot in the head and
Angel Castro whose teeth were broken on the
hood of a police cruiser before they
gunned him down at the age of 15 and
Shirley Cologne who they pushed from the
roof of a housing project with her hands
cuffed and behind her,
her body splitting the pavement into a canyon of
spilled possibility and

Moises de Jesus, beaten to death for having a seizure,
Arthur Diaz for dumpster diving,
Kenneth Fennel shot four times in the head for
driving 70 in a 65 and
Ramon Gallardo shot because swat-team members
were at the wrong address and
Robin Pratt whose tiny frame was ripped apart by
machine-gun bullets because swat team members
were at the wrong address.

And Johnny Gammage, Wayne Garrison, Malice Green,
LaTanya Haggerty, Esquiel Hernandez, Solomon Hernandez,
Felix Jorge Jr., Sean Bell, Tyisha Miller, Ramarley Graham, Paul
Childs, Oscar Grant, John Crawford, Tamir Rice, Mike
Brown…

But it's also for the Mohicans and the Chesapeake
and the Mende, the Yoruba, the Igbo, and the Hausa…

See, the mechanism's the same.
The game hasn't changed.
They'll brutalize your body and
slander your name,
black-boot stomp your door in,
shock-wave your frame,
because the boys in blue suits
think it's all in the game.

Now some of us grew up on collard greens and
cultural mythology makes us think that
victim is in our pathology
but I ascended from folk

who, in the bellies of ships,
got real good with God and transcended that shit.
So fuck the cowards who hold onto the sheep paradigm;
there's no shame in submission but
when it's time to rise, it's time.

Fuck the Sambos, the Jigaboos, the Toms and the Bucks.
Fuck the Kizzies, the Wenches, the Mammies and such.

The ones who abort their spirits but
don't have the courage to test the body
while they throw pennies in wishing wells.
I ask the strong ones to get behind me.

The formula's simple:
Touch mine, I touch back.
Cuz there're no sheep over here:
Me and mine...the wolf pack.

Mothers of Murdered Sons

> *For Mamie Till, Emmett's mother; Sabrina Fulton, Trayvon Martin's mother; and Leslie McFadden, Mike Brown's mother.*

Women, whose sons will be buried before them,
lose a lot of blood in delivery.
Their water breaks, torrentially,
their bones go soft as yolk.
Each contraction is a snatching hand,
a howl in a place you wanna rub but can't reach.
A deliberate flood.
The way a dam breaks and swallows a city.
A woman's body is like that.
It can announce a funeral better than a gunshot can.
For the women whose children are murdered,
labor is foreshadow.
It tells about the bones and the breaking and
the temporary nature of things.
Have mercy.

Mamie Till laid up nine hours tryna pull that boy
through her quaking thighs.
Sharpened her teeth on ice chips and
whispered prayers that didn't belong to anybody's God.
Nipples like church steeples,
high and hard and reaching out to sky.
Just to get that boy here.
And he was a fat thing too.
Came up grinnin' and full with himself, even then.
Came up gaspin' for air.
Came up from the thick heat of her body smackin' his lips.
Always hungry, see?

Always hungry.
Took 'em a while to clean Emmett up.
Took even longer for Mamie to stop spillin'
every bit of herself in that stark white room.
Took a while, see, and some of that blood ain't ever wash up.
Ain't that a metaphor for always?

Now, Sabrina Fulton was a ritual.
You know…stony.   Stoic.
Her face doesn't move much.
Like a closed door with too many keyholes.
No keys.
Each new sorrow a padlock welded shut.
Except her eyes keep stories even when she won't.
Ever since her youngest boy got killed
you can't look her in the eyes.
If you do, Sabrina will bewitch you with her suffering.
That ain't how she wants it, that's just how it is.
Still. Something needs to be said about how Trayvon's head
just about split Sabrina in two.
Looked like somebody was thundering out from under her
with a hatchet in his hands.
When I tell you she bled, you better know she bled.
They couldn't get it to stop.
Doctor came in bellowing, like Sabrina had
something to do with how she was coming apart.

Women keep their own magic but
you better believe God or something like it is involved
when a son is being born.
How you think a woman goes in as one, but comes out as two?
They say the last person to split himself like that

was Jesus, ain't that right?
You've been to Sunday school. You know.
Father, Son, and Holy Ghost?
Three in one. One in three?

I'm trying to say, women have always been about
the otherworldly super-terrestrial mathematics of
becoming more than themselves, since before Eve.

Sabrina almost had to have a transfusion, you know.
That boy tore her UP.
So much blood look like she didn't keep any of it for herself.
Nurses and doctors running.
Tryna stop that woman from floodin' the room
with the red paint graffiti of sons who have to get here and
can't figure how to do it without tearing something up first.
Ain't that a metaphor for always?

Now Leslie.
She doesn't come from anything that bends easily
or apologizes much.
She comes from something old.
Her people split wood, tapped trees,
picked cotton, tried it, you know.
Tried gettin' to someplace with plenty of work, and
public transportation, and enough white folk who
would look you in the eye even if it was to spit in it.
You been hungry long enough,
that's all the holy you know to look for.

Leslie wasn't one of those girls who
grew up thinking she could cry to get what she needed.

Fact is she didn't even cry when she let her firstborn
burst through her skin and he was a BIG one.
Like his daddy, I guess.
Dark. Thick-boned.
Like something made to be hunted, skinned.
Like something to be left bleeding outside.
In the middle of a road.
Caution tape all 'round.
Little kids squalling.
Old folks hollering, "Peace, Be Still" and
there Leslie was, in the thick of it all,
watching that boy she fought her own body for,
the one who barely got outta high school,
the one she alchemized from her simple womb first,
laid up circus-ing the street with his blood.
So much of it.
Just like when he was born and
the doctors had to cut Leslie to pull him through.
How HER blood got in his eye.
How it seemed like he never forgot the trauma of
inheriting a body like the one he had.
The boy whose blood started a riot.
How we all ended up with it in our eye.

The prayers of mothers with murdered sons
don't arrive in heaven anymore.
Could be they never did.
And maybe God's a charlatan pitching pennies
to the sound of black boys
breaking the world with their bleeding.
Maybe he's too busy with more righteous indignation.
Maybe the melody ain't right.

Not enough of the Eucharist in these boys to matter
to the omnipresent and
nevertheless absentee father...
Maybe he's too busy with the mothers
of school shooters and corporate fat cats
who suicide themselves
after filing for bankruptcy.
Maybe he's too busy to see he's not the only one
with a murdered son!

What about these, God? Huh?
What about these?

A Letter to Obama, Which Means Nothing

The last time I saw you,
it was June or July
in D.C., and you hadn't quit
your integrity yet.
You had pictures of your
wife everywhere and
hadn't killed Osama or
countless civilians in the Middle East

with your "smart" bombs, your drones,
your First World policies
and the Third World bodies;
your speeches were fledgling
but crisp and resounding and
people believed you.

We couldn't hear the murderer in you yet.
Could be because you were black
but not the kind of black we
can't hug or share a joke with.
Could be that your wife was so
honestly black,
not racially ambiguous,
not quietly ethnic,
but black…black for real.
Little girls in Southside Chicago
could look at her and see something
familiar, something like an auntie
that braids their hair on Saturday mornings and

makes banana pudding better
than anybody.

Could be another case
of the Emperor's New Clothes.
Could be you made us think of
Kennedy and King.
(We weren't thinking about the way they died,
just the way they made us feel.)

Could be the prerequisite for being American
is to appoint a killer to the highest office,
assign him the widest power,
give him room to wage his wars,
to ponder later what went wrong.
To leave it all to the historians
who'll tell the story of
barbarism and the complicated
business of making the world
democratic and dumb.

Could be a wicked leader's the template.
They can free-base in hotel rooms,
solicit prostitutes,
get found out and still
get re-elected.
Who can fuck their interns
in the Oval Office,
can Watergate,
manufacture crises,
arrest and detain,
search and seize and wiretap and recant,

can ignore Rwanda
but bomb the shit out of Kosovo.
They can fund apartheid
then denounce it later.
They can teach you how to
make bombs to fight Russians
but then pretend they've never seen
your face when you stop
killing Russians and start killing us.
They can feign grief and shock
when it all goes down:
      Bang Click Pop Boom.

Nuke the Japanese,
slaughter Indians,
enslave Africans,
push out Mexicans,
call war a name so
sweet it sounds like home,
sounds like righteousness,
sounds like Manifest Destiny.

But Obama, you were supposed to be different.
The Sub-Saharan African whose
bones and blood you borrow from
should have made you more conscious,
more wary,
more vigilant
(we thought);
we didn't see the Czar in you,
the Caesar in you,
the Pol Pot in you.

Could be we're not supposed to.
The anthology of American History
is the autobiography of an empire,
the memorized speeches,
the "feel your pain" rhetoric
that disarms reason and replaces it
with tyranny,
the saturation bombings,
the bodies, the bodies!

My mama voted for you, you know.
She brought all of her Jim-Crow walloped
wild imaginings to the booth and
said you were the one that could lift us out
of hell and into light.

But I met you when you were
still a senator with an office
full of pictures of your
honestly black wife,
a Kenyan walking stick, and
and pair of boxing gloves
in a case, signed by Muhammad Ali,
"The greatest of all time."

I met you back in D.C. in the summer
when the corner boys were
just a stone's throw away from
the Pentagon,
selling heroin and crack
out loud and in full view,

the constituency of the disaffected.
The ones who know better than any of us
that politics is a country of old men
and borders and war
all dressed up to look Star-Spangled,

where no light can ever reach in.

Karma

We become poets
in an attempt to tether words
to righteousness,
our notebooks
to social consciousness.

Sitting cross-legged and anxious in
wing-backed chairs we
sip lattes to news of regimes
firing American-made artillery into
crowds of folk;
their bodies pickled by the sun
line streets in countries
we never think about and
we suck our teeth and
ask a thesaurus to become a machete

and, as romantic as passivism is
these days,
I dream of dictators falling headfirst
into karma, and forget to be afraid.

If I could write this shit in fire,
        I would write this shit in fire.

This ain't poetry.
It's rage, unmuted.
A verb, a means, an end.
This is my body.
This is a sacrifice.

This is an offering.
This is Southside Chicago,
Compton, California,
Red Hook Projects in Jersey,
Roosevelt Projects in Brooklyn.

This is severed hands.
Clubs against flesh.
Black boots to pregnant bellies.
This is sterilizations.
Inoculations.
Leg irons and chains.
The bit and the noose.

This is a war cry.
Tell Massa I'm coming back
carrying fire in my knapsack.
Tell him I'm Patrice Lumumba,
Steven Biko,
Fred Hampton,
Fannie Lou Hamer,
Harriet Tubman.

Tell him they've been born again in me.

Tell him I found my mother tongue
buried under the rubble of
The World Trade Center.
Tell him this shit ain't no poem.
This is me, running naked
from sugarcane and cotton fields
having dropped my croaker sack.

Tell him he can call me karma.
I'm re-fleshing the bones.
A witch, a root-worker,
a sorceress, a priestess, a gangster...

Tell him this is the result of segregation.
Tell him this is the result of integration.
Tell him I've never been invisible.
Tell him he's never been invincible.
Tell him I'll melt the barbed wire and
steel bars of prison yards.
They'll flow over him like lava.

I'm returned.
I'm blood-thirsty.
I'm fangs and hooks and
swollen feet in welfare lines,
the gauntlet thrown down,
lines drawn in the sand.
I'm apocryphal.
Historical deletions gathering themselves
up and into textbooks.
I'm the niece of exploitation
on a rice and pancake box,
come to collect the royalties
for Aunt Jemima and Uncle Ben...

I'm a line of smoke,
a rain dance,
the tomahawk used to kill the first invader,
a passbook in South Africa,
a Whites Only sign on a courthouse door

in Mississippi,
the streets of Benghazi pocked in
prayer beads and shell casings,
the juxtaposition of faith and savagery.

Tell him I'm African wide hips and
American bulimia,
peace symbols on assault rifles.
It's the deepest kind of contradiction.

If I could write this shit in fire,
    I would write this shit in fire.

Tell Massa I'm coming back.
Howl in the wind, I'm coming back.
Bur in his heel, I'm coming back.

I'm coming back, Massa.
I'm coming back, Massa.

I'm coming back.

Birmingham Sunday

I don't know what came loose first...
A church ain't made for fallin' in on itself;
you don't build 'em prepared for destruction,
you build 'em thinkin' 'bout the praise shout,
the hand-clap, the open-mouthed communions,
how many choir members can fit in the pulpit,
the pancake breakfast you gon have in the basement and
the stained glass Jesus.
EVEN in Birmingham, Alabama 1963,
where you had to account for dynamite,
for waterlogged protest marchers
swept so clean off their feet
they fell like bloody torn right angles to
foamin'-at-the-mouth police dogs,
billy clubs and batons.

But churches ain't made for fallin' down
and I don't know what came a-loose first...
If the pillars tipped over before the pulpit shuddered,
if the windows hung for a moment in their frames
before the terrible speed of shrapnel
got in the way of everything...

If you were a colored girl in Birmingham
you knew how to duck and shrink,
how to be a misspelled word,
an incomplete sentence
squelched down to sugar softened
press-and-curl perkiness.

Their silence was so loud.
Their teeth a locked gate.
Their mouths held annual sit-ins
for their flame-red throats,

the sizzle and spill of every unsaid thing.

And it's hard to be so still
with all that playground and star-shine shimmy
in the stretch of our bones.
But on Sundays we get it near right.
The mornings roll out in hot cakes and black coffee.
Daddy's a baritone down the hall singin' hymns,
Mama's fixin' his tie, then yellin' 'bout stockings and
"Get on in here and eat before this food gets cold!"
and we can wear our hair down.
It'll be curled 'round our ears
and stopped with ribbon
and the wild hunger of Jim Crow
can't find you in church
so we slidin' 'round the kitchen in
our white shoes without a single scuff
and your sister gets to dab a little rouge
on her cheeks just on Sundays,
just on Sundays,
and the car ride is a sovereign floating joy
the whole way cuz mama can sing
and she's rollin' that pretty bell-tinkle
soprano out and we pickin' up the chorus
where we can, though
we have to keep tuggin' at our slip
so it doesn't dip below our dress...

We're everything new and shiny
that God has ever loved
and deep and high in our colored girl
sometime-loveliness
because Jim Crow didn't seek you in church.

I don't know what came a-loose first
but when the choir was singin':

"I wish I knew how it would feeeeel to be free..."

and you were a wet giggle with your sister
in Sunday school
the sky fell down and smothered everything.

Ceiling tiles flew like occasional birds
smacked the walls and smoldered...
Skulls and incandescent smoke,
a wild death for a young girl...
The crackle and pop of spinning fire
that burns everything to cinders,
a valley of broken jawbones,
baby teeth scattered like confetti,
the sun crazy with shining anyway,
the flesh insulted rubble,
the refugeed clergy diggin' through
the glass and mortar
findin' tiny limbs and

the world was a singed skirt.

I don't know what came a-loose first...

but it all came a-loose, didn't it, Addie and Denise?
Didn't it, Cynthia? Didn't it, Carole?
Didn't it all break a-loose?
Didn't it drop the winter in?
Didn't it catch and keep the sky snatched low
by the terrible clang of dynamite?

It's funny. It's a dream. And the dream's a roar
and the roar keeps time with dragons.

I don't know what came a-loose first.
Churches ain't for fallin' down.
Colored girls should be safe on Sunday.

No one should offer you a heaven
no matter how honeyed
when you hadn't even had your period yet.
Or been to your first boy/girl dance,
or had the chance to gossip about it the next day,
laughing foot-stomp wait-'til-you-hear-this whimsy
that was still your right,
no matter what Jim Crow said...

And nobody can re-flesh your bones.
Your mama will never be the same
woman who could smile with all her teeth...
Because somebody lifted a sheet
and underneath it was your bomb-blasted body
and the world broke open and swallowed her whole...

"Things fall apart.
The center will not hold" but do
you hear that?
Just over all that ugly, you hear that?
Past the thunder-crack of grief and Go down, Moses...
You hear that?
Can't no detonated handmade nothin' touch it
just over the tracks and down the street a ways
there's still hide and seek, rough and tumble,
tag and tea parties.
Some little girl's still hula-hoop and hopscotch wonderful
twirlin' 'round in her mama's old stitched and re-stitched skirts
and she's gonna go to church on Sunday singin'

"I wish I knew how....it would feeeeeel to be free...."

And mean it.
And mean it.

Because Kojo Went to War

My neighbor went to Vietnam
when he was 20 years old and
unlucky enough to
be born in 1947,
a year the draft was looking for,
same year television
came to America.

Kojo (we call him Kojo)
got drafted and before he
could thank his mama for
how hard she worked to
make sure his slacks were pressed and
his shirts were clean.
He was lifted out of Detroit and
set down in the jungle
that gorged itself on the bones of
more young men than can
ever be reckoned with,
no matter how many
statues got erected
later in their names.

In Vietnam, the air was thick
with sulfur.
Stray dogs scavenging
the junk piles for food,
they ate the bodies of
boys who had come from
Valdosta, and Chicago,

from Mississippi and Detroit.
A lieutenant, a major,
a general, a sergeant,
the enlisted salute and nod,
hup two three four:

the constant rain
the rubble
the remains
the little girl without pants
the Vietcong
the civilians
the inability to know the difference
the body parts
like souvenirs
the boys who went in
the monsters who came out
the invaders
the defenders
the inability to know the difference
the patriots
the warmongers
the inability to know the difference
the conquests
the blood-letting
the ransacking
the raping
the prostitutes
the women
the inability to know the difference
the fear
the loathing

the hubris
the ego
the artillery
the landmines
the slaughter
the mass graves
the gutted ones
the gunned down ones
the faraway funerals
that were not funerals
the shrapnel
the debris
the smoke and mirrors
the dismembered
the disremembered
two million scorched bodies
the casualties of war
collateral damage
our favorite refrain.

Kojo went in wanting things.
Went in thinking he could come out again.
Went in holding out hope for
baseball games and backyard barbecues.
Still thought he could get out as himself.
But you can't keep these things
with a gun in your hands,
your second language is cruelty.
Kojo practiced his fluency and
got the purple heart
for how quickly he learned it.

There's no way to get good with
God in a war.
A man knows his orders better
than he knows his prayers.
America awards her killers
with ribbons and parades,
stripes and bars,
the 21-gun salute.

Kojo was not a man when he
came back to Detroit.
The landmine he stepped on
killed the guy to his left and
the one to his right;
the drop-dead boys of
The United States Marine Corps
peppered the landscape
with bone meal,
the charred flesh ritual of unholy.
Hoo-Ah!

Kojo got his eye blown out of his head.
His arm practically torn off,
it flapped crazily at his side
hanging on by one meaty tendon
that wouldn't let go.

He sleeps on his rooftop now,
the neighborhood's favorite joke…
His crazy is how we feel better about
our own dumb lives.

Kojo said he thought about
swallowing a bullet,

but couldn't figure out how to do it.

He only knew how to kill the innocent.

A Poem for Coretta

There was nothing symbolic about
Martin Luther King Jr. being shot in the neck.
No metaphor could capture the sting a community felt
when yet another assassination tore at
the resolve of folks who lived in their heads and
dreamed of someday and one day…
A bullet can punctuate a movement but

I don't think about that day.

Not even when my children come marching
with images of the man embellished in crayon and
the kind of exuberance that only youthfulness and
naiveté can sustain.

They want to tell me about the dream he had and
the evil in the world that snatched it.
They run it all down for me, wide-eyed and
mortified at how helpless they feel
in these conversations with history
where great men who dared to jut out were struck down,
and the gross improprieties of it all
and the incredible immorality of it all
and the needlessness and senselessness of it all---
Can't believe how damned ungodly we were!
They need me to do something about it,
wrestle the past down to fairy tales and affix
"And they all lived happily ever after" at the end.

But I don't think about that day.
Or the man who steadied his hand,
shouldered his rifle and put Martin in his scope.
The man who woke up that morning and ate his eggs and
drank his coffee with a mission statement curdling his veins.
The man who knew he would take a life that day,
a big life,
a bigger than can be believed life
because all life is bigger than can be believed.
How he probably showered in silence
feeling powerful and intentional and
whoever loved him probably kissed his cheek and said
some casual not at all epic thing
as he was leaving, like:
"Don't forget to pick up some milk on your way out"
and how he nodded and
knew he would obligate history to remember him,
and how calculating he was,
and certain he was,
steeped in his own vast set of politics and platforms.
He set his jaw against the hubris of history
and squeezed.

But I don't think about that day.

Not that one, or the one that preceded it
when Coretta must've felt something
catch in her back that heavied her steps and
pulled her lip down,

must've gazed as she did every morning
at the man she married and been struck dumb by

how unlucky they were to be
talking out loud about freedom
and what happened when folks started believing,
and the women who hung the hopes they had
for an entire generation on the sermons of
a man she fell in love with because he made her laugh.

Not the tattered Bible, earmarked and underlined
under his arm or
the seismic impact of the words he spoke or
the swell of folk who gathered outside churches and
on corners to hear him talk of parables and possibilities,

but because he made her laugh.
A deep and rolling laughter that moved her
to girlishness and wet her mouth with smiling.

I don't think about that day.

Or the one after it
when his wife had locusts in her belly and
could see neither promised land nor
mountaintop around her children's wailing.
Their small hands pulling at her skirt,
needing her to fix it,
to tell God he made a mistake,
that daddies were supposed to be forever,
that however inevitable the newsreels reported it,
bleeding out and leaving was never an option and
the gnashing of baby teeth and the thunder-crack of
a nation's grief when
all she wanted was to remember what laughing felt like

when Martin made her do it and
what dreaming felt like
when Martin made her do it and
what faith felt like and hope felt like and
the moments that were replete with
parables and possibilities and she still believed
she could affix "And they all lived happily ever after,"

at the end.

Black Mass

> *"Then Jesus took the cup and gave it to his disciples.*
> *Take this, all of you, and drink from it…"*

The day I pretended to be Catholic
to taste the communion wine
to belong to the strange ritual
of transmogrification and wafers,

Derrick shot a six year-old
by mistake.

He bought a handgun for protection
from the gangs and their
insistent cruelties,
the afternoon bloodletting
block after block of bone meal

that never disturbed the evening cocktails
enjoyed in houses bigger than ours,
with soundproof gardens,
a handful of blocks away.

I didn't know he was going to do it.
He didn't know he was going to do it.

The gun was sudden
the way guns are.
The bullet, a concert of unholy,
found the child and held on.

The day I pretended to be Catholic
to taste the communion wafers
to belong to the strange ritual
of transmogrification and wine,

Derrick shot his best friend's little brother
by mistake.
A child he played with and knew well,
a child who died right away,
carried away suddenly and, with him,
any belief I had in prayer.

> *This is my blood.*
> *The blood of the new and everlasting covenant*
> *which has been shed for you and for all,*
> *so that sins may be forgiven.*

Midnight Bridge

For Deletha Ward

finding out about you and the way you died
      meant to remember the men who came for me,
the ones who bludgeoned,
      the ones who brought monsoons with them
each awful knuckled knowing that
      makes women go limping into flood
waters to escape the teeth.
      i don't know the names of those who
watched you being destroyed,
      the ones who didn't help,
who didn't offer their own bodies,
      the ones who stood still as you leapt
from a bridge into the clutching dark
      of the detroit river.
a river with too many secrets.
      I've wanted to give them death names,
to call for their heads on spikes,
      their own limp limbs dangling wetly
from a midnight bridge, but they're
      too many to kill.
i know how it happens,
      how good people don't move when
you're stripped and flayed.
      the fascination of flesh.
the way it comes so easily apart.
      to watch is better than to know,
to marvel and to shudder
      but not to help or say enough.
lynch parties only form to kill the innocent.

        they don't know how to insist on a woman's
right to the world.
        we're familiar when we're bleeding,
when we're a caterwauling stretch of open-mouthed
        anguish...
hundreds of people attended my stepfather's funeral
        but no one came to mine, deletha.
i was forced to bury myself.
        this is the way it happens.
the way our dying is tradition,
        the way the destroyer keeps his teeth.
the crowds don't move.
        how your daughter must hate the
sound of shorelines.
        how she wakes up gnashing her teeth.
your mother will raise her to eulogize you right.
        she'll live for as long as she can
motherless and knowing.
        her own death
will somehow
        be similar.
she'll be like the rest of us.
        she'll learn how to bury herself.
        if she's lucky
there'll be no crowd
        to watch.

A Requiem for Renisha

Detroit doesn't know how to hold
a black girl, gentle.
It's the invention of sorrow.
A theatre of abandoned
buildings, a willful city
of ghosts and murder.

I know you wandered into
this life with your
fists out.
Named the dolls you never got
after girls you knew who died
in the hell days of growing long bones
in a slaughter-house city
where geography is proof of curses.

A city that teaches one awful lesson
after another:
> a girl can be shot in the face,
> a girl who asked for help,
> who knocked on the wrong door
> and was met with a shotgun,
> whose impromptu life
> oozed out in the morning
> in a Detroit suburb.

The curfew of blackness
is to suffer the streetlight,
to try to get home before
they come on.

To pose for photos that
will be used by cops
when your mama has to
identify your body.

To watch your own funeral procession
from the dustbin of history...
    to concede
    to accept
    to endure.
Always, always endure.
Umbilical relationships

        to nooses.

Oh America…

I went out looking for
what you promised and
found a toothless grin,
an empty pot,
boneyard lullabies,
sweet-less shores,
witches burned to cinder,
little black girls bombed
in churches,

they are all me.

Each charred bone,
each torn dress
is the story of my birth.

I'm a wandering ghost here.
This mud-struck bitch
pledging allegiance
to the pitchfork,
stupidly sturdy anyhow,

my Easter dress,
my winding cloth.

You tried to kill me.
Made my death tradition.
Ohhhh, but I'm stubborn in this skin.
It doesn't matter what weapons
you point:

I roll the stone away,
outlast death,
abandon it in the
cause of my name,
my holy,
my righteous name.

What will you do, America?
What can you do with
this cliff-hanging colored girl
who pioneered
her own dumb body
despite the ambulance ride
you turned things into?
See how incurably permanent I am.

See how these skeletons
tumble out of my mouth.
The grisly burst of unnamed
corpses that hang above my head.
A halo of deliberate memory.

Oh America,
you put a war in my veins.
Hoped I'd die from the poison
or be disappeared by debris,

but I grew past the
bile and carry too many
grave-jumpers in my
photo album to succumb to
your kind of death ritual:

1619 was this morning.
I can feel the first cargo of
trembling Africans
fighting to keep their names
in a place too indulgent in
blood sport.

They are all me.

Each one is me.
I have inherited a swarm
of bees for blood.

What will you do, America?

What cemetery can you build
for a girl so full of memory?

Bodies are Only Bodies

For example, the time
those two boys threw
five-year old Eric out
of a window at Cabrini Green
when Cabrini Green was
still Cabrini Green:

boarded windows,
rotting garbage stacked in
clogged trash chutes,
gangland graffiti announcing
murder just down from
the corner of Locust & Sedgwick
that the neighborhood called the Death Corner
cuz fifty people died in the exact
same spot in the stretch of a year,
and the Vice Lords and
the Gangster Disciples, and

Little Dantrell shot in the face
on the way to school and
Shatoya Currie
(you haven't heard of her)
the nine-year old girl
who was raped and beaten,
insecticide sprayed in her mouth,
her throat crushed under her
attacker's boot heel
in the stairwell not far
from her apartment, leaving her

paralyzed, blind and mute.

What happened to her was
just what happened to her.
There's no greater meaning
than that in a place
swollen with doom and
inevitable demolition,

bodies are only bodies
when you live in the projects.

North side Chicago is a dystopian alternate universe
where the monsters look like
boys in baggy jeans,
motherless and Titanic.

They're starving so they're violent.
Murder is how you announce your suffering
when no one's listening,
when the bodies are only bodies,

when the weight of your heart
is the corroboration with fallen sky,
when the block you grow up on
is desecrated by the blood of

folk who look just like you.
Each mirror reflection a snarling
reminder that you'll die this way too,

unrecorded, yes, and unremarkably lost,

summoned to hell from the moment
of your birth.

A punishment for the sin of being
born at all.

The Sons of Oil Men

Legacies are important so
let them be what they are.
Fathers with money are the
keepers of the gate.
They hold the flood beneath
their feet.
Titan-like they attach their names
to everything.
They know how to keep from drowning.
How to give their sons
keys and manifests
they lay out capitalistically:

Here, son. The spoils of war. Your inheritance…

And George…the damnable part?
The damning, unknowable part?

You and Osama?
Same hands.
Same castle of blood.
Same fat pockets.
The singular fruit:
Twin boys,
the ratio of gun to gluttony,
mansion to massacre,
two crows on razor wire,
grand wizards of electrocution,

butchers with hand grenades and
the best red wine.

Osama and George sittin' in a tree
K- I- L- L- I- N- G...

And the nursery rhyme
falls ill to the original story.
It's an old, old knowing
the Cain and Abel ritual---
Two brothers, one generation
shy of God,
divested from piety
pulling down paradise
fist by fist.
See those birds in the oil slick,
their wings gleaming black
like a widow's funeral dress.

That's the legacy of empires.
This is what oilmen leave their sons.

Apple tree is bloodroot
OR
Apple tree is skyscraper.
Metaphor---either way---for murder.

There never was an apple tree,

only boys
pulled irreligiously from the womb
of simple women and

handed a kingdom.

Seeking sin…

Finding it.

On the Subject of Eve

Let one more man
defile a woman and
I grow horns in her name.

Who are these Pharaohs?
They are unpeople
handing switchblades to their sons.
The scripture robbers
who rewrote Eve as unholy
afterthought, a borrowed rib
defying God in the garden.

Be still with these lies.
The mythology of woman
bringing ruin is only partially right:
        We've awakened
        the dragon in our blood.
Our blood,
        a banner of quiet scheming.
Our scheming,
        the bastard child of battle.

You cooked up the thick sin of authorship,
illustrated her without mercy,
a woman born not of woman,
The God Queen
who ached from shadows
until she ruptured volcanically.
Saw Adam for what he was,
kept the company of snakes,

her husband's rib a rotting harp
in her impossible body.

The music she made
biting into that fruit,
stentorian for the daughters
who followed...

Gladiator Sorcery

For Assata Shakur

What's left to say, Assata?
You're Daniel
Improbably freed from the lion's den
To eat overripe mangoes,
Sip your tea
And host occasional company
In your modest apartment
In Havana.
Cuba's always been
A welcome sign above the door
For the revolutionary.

The FBI wants your bones
Still
This isn't new.
The monster's always hungry.
The cannibal heart of politics
Can't bear to lose
To a woman.

You're Nat Turner forgetting sleep,
Toussaint L'Ouverture rupturing the grave,
His mud-borne knuckles
Snatching resurrection into
Your wild, wild bones.

You showed them how willful a
Woman can be when she
Knows the topography of

Her freedom,
When the landscape's the
Beating of her heart,

An arena of gladiator sorcery,

Assata, you're mighty because you're alive.
The one who got away,
A bedtime story I tell my own daughter
To pray her hands into fists.

No ode is right enough, Assata.
We've traveled the distance
Of our own imagination
To earn the torchlight you put in us.
Your name is prophecy
That we can get off our front porch,
That the lion's den can be defied,
That we can escape with our hands.

You show us, Assata,
Our heroes don't have to give by dying.

You show us how to chew through the rope.

Brave goddess with a smile that rides
The dizzy surges of your blood,
Would-be malarial witch,

Deliver us into insurrection.

Improbable Bird

For Elaine Brown, Chairman of the Black Panther Party

It couldn't have been easy, moon woman,
Not easy at all for you
        To talk down your nature and
        Wear a general's armor,
        To fascinate your flesh by

Giving it bigger names,
To be the chairperson of
        So despised an army of
        Black men in black leather
        Holding rifles, patrolling the streets
Of Oakland
        They practically levitated
        With wild intention

                And you, the improbable bird
                      With impeccable lineage,
                      A line of proper ladies
                      Decorating your pretty pedigree,

You were supposed to grow up to
Be one of them,
        To imprison your wanderlust
        In favor of a husband and
        A job that asked of you high heels
        And long skirts, but you
Knew something about the madness
That revolutionaries have to keep.
        You listened for the crack of the whip

    And heard it,
The blood anthem of imperialism,

        And you, appallingly weary from it all,
           Your long bones rebelling against
           Church clothes and quiet,

You took up arms under the
Trumpet of stars
And promised a resistance,
    A conjurer's savage faith
    In men,

    And victory.

Haiti, My Heart

The sky in Haiti's a stretch of black gold.
The stars blanket the ubiquitous fervor
of occasional tourists and Red Cross workers
armed with malaria pills and
missionary zeal.

Haiti's a synonym for ruin,
the heavy price paid
for killing slave masters.

This unblessed island,
the inherited mother of
rebellious Africans who
didn't waste the
night with dreaming.

In Saint-Domingue
God's an orange moon.
Our names: the scorched earth,
                  the sugarcane on fire,
                  the coffee plantations,
                  the indigo too.
Seagulls carried
burnt limbs in their beaks:

The carrion song of revolt,

the sweet meat of corpses
rode the salt water
better than Christ

and far more biblically.
Brain matter like spoiling bananas
littered the shore,
popping from unrelenting heat.

The women grew scales that day.
The mermaid, witchcraft.
Blood steamed their bones
like a runaway train,
the vodou rumpus of exotic battle
steaming the island to sulfur.

Haiti, the death dirge
that sings me home,
the dream of extra-terrestrial strength,
the heart obeying itself:
An island made of chains,
the bones of slain men,
fallen angels orbiting The Citadel,
the prehistoric tribe of
an eye for an eye.

Pitched soundlessly against
the roaring tide,

the hiss of Never Again.

Send an SOS to the President

Tell him we're under attack
cuz apparently he don't know.

The woeful murder-heavy streets
caterwaul the walloped bodies,

the filth of fascist theatre
gobbles the epileptic morning,

a blue/black movement
sprung loose on a narrow
street in Ferguson, Missouri,
a place ain't nobody even heard of
'til the death-knell August siren of
Mike Brown's face down
concrete funeral procession.

Big ol' electric Negro like
John Henry with sledgehammer fists
ghosted now, and this,
---no ballad of remembrance---,
the gunmetal mockingbird
beating his beak bloody in a cage
freed now I guess from
his moon-struck skin.

A black magnolia wilted in autumn
on a Saturday
plunged to godlessness,
the foretold martyr

like every other black boy before him,
song so old it's a player piano of
die nigga diiiiieeeee.

The intrusion of mothers
at crime scenes is spectacle
down in the deep of it:
They've hysterical (historical?) ties
to fallen sons,
their grief is coliseum,
the crooked radiance of
women coming apart,
the undeep ritual of stoning.

That bird overhead's imitating
winter, pay it no mind.
The cops are still here and
they won't leave 'til we're
a traveling circus of successful
suicide attempts.
They're practicing for the big show.
The finale's a doozy!

A carnival of amputated hands:
the boys are beheaded on Monday,
the girls mutilated on Tuesday,
old folk are used for target practice,
their soupy bones surrender
deliciously quick,
the babies are fed to the wolves.

I said, the babies are fed to the wolves.

They don't even spare the babies.
Our flamboyant blood entrances them,
it pirouettes to Negro Spirituals,
resplendent ballerina blood
they use to paint the army barracks.

The Homecoming of vultures and barren fields,
they'll climb out of morality
every morning and do it again.

The carnival of amputated hands:
the boys are beheaded, that's Monday,
the girls mutilated on Tuesday,
old folks are used as targets,
the babies fed to the wolves.

There's nothing to see here.
Mike Brown died.
We got tickets to the show.
We're dumb with waiting

for the crack of the whip to
signal riot.

I'm a miscarriage of
unfertilized fruit trees.
A mouth full of evil
on a midnight ride,
blind from the smoke and
can't find my own children.
They're eating their insides

the way hyenas do
when they've been eviscerated.
The plunder of taking hard medicine.
They're looting themselves
for a cotton-candy waltz.

I can't get to them.

Blood in my eye.

Chain Gang

This song is not a language.
Not a thing to be remembered,
The field-holler tradition of
Teeth and knees
Cursing wind,
A concert hall of bloody hands
Spilling the earth,
Strangling dirt,
Sledgehammer curses
Of men busted open.

On Parchman Farm
You could hear it coming
Up through the trees
The hammering pulpit of
Crooning men and sweat,
The tender meat of palms
Pulped like plums.

Them men gulped down the
Dawn dew air,
Let it catch in their throats,
Broke the sunrise up and
Sang hymns like hexes:

Be my woman, gal, I'll beeee your maaaaaaan…

And the killing fields of Mississippi
Fizzled down to juke joints and
The hothouse music of illegal clubs

With thick women they loved outright and
Played cards with and
Gave bourbon to when their hands
Didn't hold sorrow like
Pick axes and the railroad was
Just a railroad,
A way to ride north if you could
Get your money right.

Redbone gals with rose-water sweat,
When they lifted their knees
Sunflower County was a heaven
They believed in.

Stick to the promise, gal, that you maaaaaade meeeeee…

Steady now,
They turned back the clock on
Their hard, hard hands,
Let the memory of fresh linen and
Ladies' slips like gossamer
Wings, a parade of plump thighs,
The juju thrust of furious bones
Spread like grease
Across starched-white sheets,
Midwife them out of ol' Parchman Farm.

And back to the cockfights and gambling,
Back when they had ambition,
Back when they had a sweet woman
To hold, her fat wrists
Soft as butter,

Limp as rain.

When she walk, she reel and rock beeeeehind
Ain't that enough to make a convict smiiiiiiiile.

Mississippi's where the cock crowed,
A hoodwink if ever there was one,
But see how a man can make a
Steeple outta his hands,

See how he can break away
From his hurt and be God
If he wants to,
How he can keep his mind
Wrapped in yesterday,
Drown out memory
Like rain drumming
Down like hornets
Yeahhhhhh.

Them Parchman men,
Ants in single file,
Draft dodgers
Digging trenches,
Pounding concrete,
Laying tracks,
Pretending it's Christmas
So they can keep their hands
Away from the colic of axe handles,
The sputtering earth
Snarling under their feet.
Warden says Every man

Gotta pay his way on Parchman Farm
Same as the outside.

Yessuh. They remember what it was like to be a man,
To know that didn't mean put a gun in your hand
Or go lookin' for somebody to take down, naw.
They sang 'til the hurt was just an
Experiment in forgetfulness and they
Were back in clean clothes makin' plans and

Tryin' to get a little money
To buy tobacco and
A pint with a little left over
To get somethin' sweet
For the women who were wet
Underneath them, crooning
A tumor-less midnight.

The moans of wild women
Are specific:
A whisper of hell danced pink
By the rose-water sweat and mewling,
Questions they ask when
Their clothes are off.

When you gon' take me to the movies?
    We goin' Saturday, baby
When you gon get you a steady job?
    Workin' on it everyday, baby
Why you love me anyway, man?
    Ain't a man alive who could help it

The dance, you know, the dance of being a free man
That never shows its fullness to you 'til
It's stripped down and gobbled up
By railroad tracks and guards in high towers
With rifles watching your back,
Bend to question mark
Under a sun that won't mind its business.

When the only part of your living life left
Is in the things you remember
About a woman who hung
Pantyhose off her porch to
Dry and made you peach cobbler
In the middle of the night
If you asked nice and
Danced with you to songs
Written on the back of a
Watermelon truck by folk who
Knew something about longing,
And those are the songs you give her now
While you bust the earth open.

Cuz your heart is a burial plot
So stony.

Can't ask nothin' of a grave.
Everybody knows that.

So you dig and
Pound and
Snatch and
Haul and

Scape and
Lift and
Tote and
Hammer.

                Lay it down, man!
                        Pick it up again, man!

You're knuckles and
Dreams deferred in a place
Where every stone,
Every goddamn stone
Is important!

I go free, lawd, I goooooooo free…..

For Margaret Garner (28 days free until)

When the sun's pitiless
When the girl's a gust of get out fast
When the boys are forced to mingle with the forest
When the baby, still nursing, leaves her mother
When the mother's the emphasis of fever
When massa's asleep to the heat
When the dogs bit the breasts off the last gal that ran
When the boys who brought her back think it's funny
When the plantation's a renaissance of sizzling flesh
When hell's a white man with a gun in his hand
When hands are the language of monsters
When the missus is a frenzy of lineament
When the mother's held down in a barn
When the baby in her belly is a choir of knives
When the water of her body's unfathomably deep
When her body's rebellious land
When massa's a real-life flood
When the babies make it over the river
When they burn another man until he pops
When the women hide their eyes but know the stench
When the wind wouldn't kiss the trees
When the dogs are lunching on wounded men
When God's a three-personed lie
When the mother climbs the air, decides to run
When the trees are Trojan horses mocking moonlight
When the trees are a funeral-pyre theatre
When her feet catch every shard that ever was
When she will not dare to feel it running faster
When the baby in her belly is no nightingale

When the baby in her belly plunges down
When the high grass of Kentucky is a manger
When the mother bore the small noun soundlessly
When the wild deer knows to nibble, a wild orchestra
When tomorrow's fantastically close
When the river's a sudden hallelujah
When the mother's a deluge, blood and milk
When the mother's a consonant of mud
When the mother finds dry land, calls it Ohio
When the mother and the wild deer ghost their chains
When the next 28 days are salve and sweet bread
When the next 28 days are chamomile
When the mother fits four babies on her lap
When her arms are measureless, a sacred rope
When the 29th day will hold no mercy
When massa proves the hell he's born to keep
When massa finds the mother with full hands
When massa is Kentucky in Ohio
When massa comes with guns and snapping dogs
His hands the rotting planks of slave ships
Left to crumbling mast-less hulls on muddy creeks,

When everything is red and fat with no
When the mother grabs her babies and a handsaw
When the mother pushes them inside a shed
When she bashes in the boys' skulls with a shovel
When she drags the handsaw's teeth across the toddler's throat
When massa stops her before she kills the newborn
When he looks at her and sees a new conceit
When the mother's eyes have gone out of her head
When she's no more a woman, no more no more,

When Margaret Garner escaped from slavery
She sent her oldest three children ahead of her,
Gave birth to her fourth along the way.

When Margaret Garner got around the water
    When she couldn't hear the rattling of chains
    When Kentucky was a trail of smoke behind her,
When she couldn't read the sheet music of lynching
When her babies played like they had freedom papers
    When 28x24 makes a promise,

When massa crossed the river thinking he knew her
    When massa stole all color from the sky,

When Margaret Garner was a carousel of heat
When she outraced massa to a murder
When the sacrilege of getting to the crucifixion first

Is a mother with milk-heavy useless breasts
And no wild deer left

To nibble.

Strange Fruit

For Emmett Till

"Southern trees bear a strange fruit.
Blood on the leaves and blood at the root."

In this photo he's laughing and
there's no cotton gin tied 'round his waist.
He's not stretched into swollen limbs.
His eyes are still hazel and
recognizable, two neat white rows of perfect teeth
sit totem-like in his mouth and
the world didn't know him because
he'd not been murdered yet.

He's still slipping into the kitchen to
get another piece of cornbread
while his mama ain't lookin'.
He'll mash it with his fingers,
drink some buttermilk and laugh
with his eyes and they're still hazel
and bright like stars in uppercase and
ain't nobody gouged 'em out
or shut 'em closed and when he goes
to school he'll do a silly dance with his
arms and legs cocked out in odd angles and
his classmates will laugh and there'll
be no cotton gin tied 'round his waist.

"Pastoral scenes of the gallant south,

the bulging eyes and the twisted mouths…"

In this photo he's proud of the hat on his head.
You can see that by how straight his neck is
and his mama's in the picture and they got the same
face and his head's high and perfect and
ain't no bullet in it and it'll be months before there is one
and in those months he's his mother's child,
the smug and overfed man-child all southern
women love to cook for and dote on cuz he
licks the plate clean even if it's leftovers.
He just eats and yes ma'ams and makes you giggle
so much you got to shoo him out the kitchen
just so you can get the pots clean and
he's breathing and whole and
ain't no men dressed like midnight with
yellow teeth and sunless un-laughing eyes
snatching him out the door
changing everything when neither of 'em
asked to be anything other than
laughing in the kitchen with
the greens still simmering in the pot.

"Here is a fruit for the crows to pluck…"

This last photo's a holocaust.
The one history concretized into
the nighttime musings of black children
who hopscotched above and below the bible belt,
who saw a tattered other worldly version of
the 14 year-old Emmett,
his head poised strangely above a sharp black suit on

the cover of Jet magazine.

There were no eyes, smiling
mischievous man-child wonderful,
cornbread and buttermilk slicking,
fast talking, looking like his mama,
bubblegum pop saunter and sizzle
straight necked full of tomorrow's boy
staring back into the camera.

What was there, wasn't there at all.
What was there, swallowed the world.
My mama was eight years old when
they painted Emmett Till's fractured image
on the cover of a negro magazine.
Eight years old.
Pigtails, knee socks, pinafores, pleats, and
a heap of pretty girl possibilities.

But I know my grandmother set that book down
with intention on the coffee table
knowing her baby girl would see it and know
what shouldn't be known but what must be known.

This is what the south did with an adolescent mistake
when a fast-talking, finger-snapping negro from up north
whistles and boasts about big city white girl honeys
with rosy lips and no Jim Crow.

It's an image I shoved

at my 13 year old son,
frenetic in my attempt to tell him
that this is black history.

I need him to know that if he isn't
careful, not brave, not the sum total of all
our unlit courage, if he relegates
these stories to cliff-notes,
he'll bleed out and die in the epilogue.

I need you to know, Salih,
that my arms will never be wide enough
to cover sins like these,
that your head held so high
is still a cautionary tale
but to go on and do it anyway and
laugh and dance with your
arms and legs cocked out in odd angles and
slip by me and get the extra cornbread
whenever you can and
be grateful that when you and your boys
say something slick
about the pretty blonde girl
in the front row of algebra...

You're permitted that levity
after 400 years of
midnights. Necks decorated in nooses.
Plantations that decorated terrorism in
white pillars and mint juleps.
I tell my son to remember Emmett Till,

to remember when his eyes
were still hazel, still smiling
and how high he held his head
to celebrate that brand new hat,
to remember that his mother loved him
and almost couldn't recognize him
after that last whistle left his throat.

I tell him I'll be his mother
and celebrate his brown boy buoyancy
all the days of my life, and that while I don't
know what tomorrow holds,
I know that he'll never be strange fruit,
will never be broken open, will never be strung up,
will never be hog tied,
will never have his face so like my own
crushed or mangled or hatcheted.

I tell my son:

I'm growing these limbs to get
'round him and surround him and
we'll be strong and
unapologetically black for as long

as we can be.

The Road That Was a Wolf

For James Byrd

(Ohhhhhh death....)

It's late. And James Byrd
Is trying to get home.
It ain't so late that he
Shouldn't be able to
But it's late and
He's walking on a road
Fresh out the juke joint
Where he's been decorating
The night with blues riffs and
Shots of whiskey,
Sweating ladies with wide
Backsides whispering sex
In his ear, and he might've
Took one of 'em up on it
But he knew better than to
Be drunk and with his pants
Down 'round his ankles in
Some lonely woman's house
After midnight.
A man does that and it's
The same thing as a
Promise and he didn't
Wanna make none.

So he put on his cap,
Thanked the bartender and
The band and got on that road

Headed home...
In Jasper, Texas
With those azaleas and sycamores
Heavy with sugar and heat.
Mockingbird molten feathers
Peppered the road.

And that road?
Well, that road dreamed
It was a wolf.
It practiced a wild hunger.
Sees James Byrd and
Sharpens its teeth.

The right kinda white boys come along.
They laaaaugh and spill their beer.
The foam sits in their whiskers,
Puddles under their feet.

This ain't no story to pass on but
James Byrd was fresh out the juke joint, see?
Still thinking he could be somebody.
He didn't know about the road or
The hunger it kept,
He didn't know about the white boys
With their scarred knuckles and chains.
He wore his good shirt that night and
The watch his mama gave him,

But James was coming apart.
A jigsaw of coulda-been and
Never-again.

Everything was the spine-bone circus
The tail-bone scrape
The razored elbow
The ripping skin
Tendons pulled clean out the flesh
Like streamers at a party you
Don't get to leave.

Whatever was pink inside
Whatever thrummed
Whatever pulsed
Got a good dragging,
Miles and miles of bone meal.

The road was a wolf.
It knew it had been.
The white boys bayed at the
Dawn-limp moon.
James Byrd couldn't get
The burn to stop:
He's pulled behind the truck,
The chains bit anklebone to shrapnel,
The blood-dazzled dirt drank and drank.

James Byrd could hear his daddy tell him
    Keep your head, man. Keep your head...
And he's trying.
The white boys don't stop
The bloodletting.
It's their favorite kind of music.
A ticker tape of soft tissue,

The clawed-out wet of torn limbs
Splintered to rhythmless clumps
Of muscle and bone.

They finally hit a culvert,
The steep pipe crescendo
That forgets God and
The allover heat went out.

The road licked the severed limbs clean.
The blood-bone ritual of unholy…

The white boys bayed at the moon.
They laaaaûghed and spilled their beer.
The foam settled into their whiskers.

This is how you talk politics in Texas:
A chain
A black man
A bludgeoning.

A Choir of Blackbirds

For Marissa Alexander

The blood of black women is unremarkable.
Window dressing, you might call it
For the horror show of lugging around
A body built for a funeral.

> Marissa met a man who
> Killed her in fractions,
> Parceled out her flesh
> Like some maggot-ridden doll.

Every weekend he sawed her in half,
The incredible disappearing lady
Pummeled under his ordinary hands;
She put herself back together each morning.

> Owned her hunger
> Like cattle waiting to be eaten,
> Kept blood clots like small children
> Obligingly heavy with a broken man's hell.

But dragons will pretend to be lambs,
Monsters will pretend to be men.
Marissa kept passing by her own red heart
Her wings fastened under his boot.

> Quiet daughter dreary with quiver,
> An unrehearsed life,
> An imaginary mouth,
> Terrible heart in a crowded house.

Her blood a choir of blackbirds,
She tunneled her own deathbed
Became the tourniquet,
Her fists a stone corsage.

    She practiced the end of him,
    Her favorite good night dream:
    Unflesh the monster and
    Leave the lights on…

She fired a warning shot,
The only grace left in her,
An SOS signal to other women like her
Fighting for their water to break.

    What can a brute do with an ocean?
    What good are his fists to the rising tide?
    He's no more a man
    Than a woman's a flea.

For swatting
Marissa, and her unoiled bones,
A sudden sacrament of steam
And water won't wait for you to learn its depth.

    It'll salt your unlearned body,
    Christen you conquered,
    Bury you mercilessly
    Beneath its cold, wide skirt.

A Child Soldier Speaks…

War's what boys are for.
I'm an orphan with
hand grenades.
I can't speak over the glint
of steel.
There's no language for this.
This curse of a thousand years
that built a city of unblessed blood.
The black-mass blotting
of my name.

I'm bewitched.
Unfamiliar to God,
I murder freely in the temple.
There's no one left to stop this,
this skeletal country of
diamond mines and refugees,
militiamen pepper the riverbanks.
We pick a girl out and
take her 'til she minces.
Her husband must watch.

This is war so you take the women.
You empty your clip in her stupid womb.
See how long she writhes.
Put her son's hand in the pulp of it.
Tell him to laugh while he digs a hole.

I like the ooze, you know.
The way they tremble

when they see you coming.
I like the feel of the gun in my hand.
It is my only certain home.
I would murder Christ for a beer.
I would!
There's no heaven for people
who die here in this.
This bomb-snatched
monsoon of misery.
Count your children.
How many are missing?

They say I had a mother once.
They say she died screaming.
They say I'm the one that did it.
That I married her brain with a machete
after four men climbed on my sister.
They say they say I had a sister.
They say my father tried to fight them.
They say they say they saw my
hands and knew I could
pick up a blade.
Made me swing it down hard into
my mother, they say they say
I had a mother but
didn't flinch when I made her

a pile of junked bone.

They say I'm a dead heart.
Was it ever alive?
Did I ever love anything

besides this gun in my hand?
Did I know a full stomach?
Was I ever without the mud from
mass graves on my hands?
Was I born?
Was I?
Was I?
Or did I show up one
morning with marching orders
hacking off the limbs
of people they say I knew.
Did I know them?
Did I?
Did I?

Has there ever been
a sunrise without
a dead girl?

This is war
and war is for boys
with steady hands.
Boys who are not boys
with no use for
a mother
or a heart

or memory.

September 2001

I lived down the street from
the North American Aerospace Defense Command.
My oldest son celebrated his 3rd birthday
three days before it happened,
the twins were potty training,
my mama 60 miles away
in a condo for school teachers,
My sister plowing through paperwork
at her corporate job downtown.

Was I partnered then?
It's hard to say.
I don't remember feeling
loved in any intimate way.
I'm sure my marriage was over.
I was alone with the children,
I know that much.
My phone was off on purpose,
I was combing my hair.
It was down to my waist then,
strangers loved to walk up
and touch it
without permission.

But anyway
I was home
when it happened,
sitting on the edge of
the tub thinking about the
white woman in Texas who

murdered her five
children three months before,
when I heard that
I was a sudden suicide.

I never told anybody about that.

How I dreamed
of her babies going blue
in that bathtub,
and how they loved her
even as their eyes bulged,
their green veins summoned
to the surface and
feces and vomit
swirling in their hair
and how the last one,
the oldest one,
fought her to the end,

how she left him in the tub
floating facedown in
shitty water.
The other four she lifted
to the bedroom,
placed them all on clean
white sheets,
all but the first
who was the last…

But anyway
that's what I was doing

when it happened.

I was thinking about dead babies,
blue white babies and their crazy
mama who I identified with
too much to acknowledge
without dreaming of dragging
a razor against my wrist.

I thought about how mad
you have to be to do it
and if you knew it
when you became it,
or if it snuck in without
warning or nobility
and the next day you
woke up and started digging
tiny graves in the garden.

So anyway,
when it happened
I was living just down from
the North American Aerospace Defense Command Center
thinking about the woman in Texas
who murdered her children,
and suicide and my own children
when I heard that two planes
hit two towers in
New York City.
I turned on my television
in time to see a man jumping
headfirst from a window in a

white button-down shirt and
dark dress slacks,

and fire and smoke and
soot all over everything and
women screaming and men
running and everyone
an open-mouthed anguish.

I sat and watched the world burn
with my children in my lap
thinking about the falling man
and the mother in Texas and
her blue, drowned babies.

The green veins in my wrist
snarling up at me, mocking:

What will you do now?
What will you do?

This is Before…

This is before mega churches and
hyper evangelical phooey
against homosexuals and heathens and
abortion, shit like that.

When you went to church
for the music
not cuz God had gotten around
to thinking about you yet
but because as far as you
were concerned prayer
was a black woman in a
long white robe singing
hymns that fixed all your crazy and

for six minutes or so
you weren't cursed at all and
didn't metabolize your grief
into medicine cabinets and
switchblades.

No, this is before telethons
with slick-haired,
fast-talking preachers
got syndicated and
interrupted the sway of
your hips on Sunday morning.

Cuz you didn't watch
those Bible shows or know about

the folly of it all, you just
loved singing in the choir and
the pipeline between you and
whatever else was out there
beyond your reach,
ignoring you on weekdays.

When you think about it
from your now cynical perch,
you sometimes miss what it
was like to be lost to logic and
swept up by the alto section
that told your heart there were
no mistakes on earth,
some goodly spirit
was rooting for you,

a far off ghost
in the abstract who
knew you by name,
didn't hold your flimsy faith
against you and

leaned forward in his throne
whenever black women
got together on
Sunday morning
to sing.

Bad Blood

For Whitney Houston and her daughter Bobbi

I blame Hollywood but
no one listens when you say
shit like that.

And now…

No spell and
no prayer for   this

         All decay usurps
             the sun

That's the bad blood
you were worried about, Whitney

         after the miscarriage and
         pregnant for the second time

that's the legacy
you feared most:

         Will she inherit my stupid heart?
         Will she dream of diving off a midnight bridge?
         Will she love that dream more
             than the one about her living?

Daughters always keep the
things we throw   away.

They can't help it.
They're how we know we're broken.

In the deep of it
this is the house you built
where nothing heroic happens,

    just the decadent decrying of hands and
    second chances.

Mother and daughter
strange apparitions floating dismally
    down

This is the legacy of stardom
    a photo album of empty eye-sockets
    the young and sometimes beautiful
    dancing dope and Old Testament dread

craving the counting of stars and
    the company of folk
    who can push you into daylight
    when you are dumb with midnight.

No one's ready for your suicide
but they always say they saw it coming
in the interviews that happen later,

    call it tragic and inevitable,
    pretend they knew the empty you kept.

They're the ones you couldn't call
on nights when you were
stained-glass windows in
a burned-out church,

>when your neck couldn't survive
>the weight of your head
>the way you tried to keep it up
>for camera flashes,

when you were a tabloid cover story,
a leaked photograph,
a disgruntled employee's exclusive interview,

a mantelpiece heavy with trophies for
songs you could no longer sing
in the same key,
in that same way when you
believed the words cuz
the melody was foraging for
your name,

when all the pictures of you in the paper
show a woman with no wild left,

>when your fan mail went unopened
>for a year,

when you couldn't call home anymore,

when the people who love you
aren't enough to keep you tethered

to the body,
your bones shingle-loose
like a bagful of nickels,

when the water wants to keep you,
when you can't help but oblige it.

    Heavy women who hearken to heaven,

don't let the water be troubled, sisters,
    by this, your premature offering,

        don't let tomorrow go without
        an afterlife at least,

don't forget the promises a body
    makes when it agrees to be a body,

both of you interrupted by

a long tradition of
    testing the flesh…

going

    going

        gone.

The Period Poem

Dude on twitter said:

"I was having sex with my girlfriend when
she started her period.
I dumped that bitch immediately."

Dear nameless dummy on Twitter:

You're the reason my daughter cried funeral tears
When she started her period.
The sudden grief all young girls feel
After the matriculation from childhood and
The induction into a reality that they'll have to negotiate
People like you and you're disdain
For what a woman's body can do.

Herein begins an anatomy lesson infused with feminist politics
Because I hate you.

There's a thing...called a uterus.
It sheds itself every 28 days or so
Or in my case every 23 days
(I've always been a rule breaker).

I digress.

That's the anatomy part.

The feminist politic part is that women
Know how to let things go,
How to let a dying thing leave the body,
How to become new,
How to regenerate,
How to wax and wane not unlike the moon and tides,
Both of which influence how YOU behave.

I digress.

Women have vaginas that can speak to each other.
By this I mean, when we're with our friends,
Our sisters, our mothers,
Our menstrual cycles will actually sync the fuck up.
My own vagina is mad influential.
Everybody I love knows how to bleed with me.
(Hold onto that, there's a metaphor in it).

But when your mother carried you,
The ocean in her belly is what made you buoyant,
Made you possible.
You had it under your tongue when you burst through her skin,
Wet and panting from the heat of her body,
The body whose machinery you now mock on social media,

THAT body wrapped you in everything
That was miraculous about it and sang you
Lullabies laced in platelets
Without which you wouldn't have a twitter account
At all, motherfucker.

I digress.

See, it's possible we know the world better
Because of the blood that visits some of us.
It interrupts our favorite white skirts and
Shows up at dinner parties unannounced.

Blood will do that.

Period.

It will come when you're not prepared for it.

Blood does that.

Period.

Blood's the biggest siren and
We understand that blood misbehaves.
It doesn't wait for a hand signal or a
Welcome sign above the door.

And when you deal in blood
Over and over again like we do,
When it keeps returning to you,
That makes you a warrior and
While all good generals know not to discuss
Battle plans with the enemy
Let me say this to you, dummy on Twitter:
If there's any balance in the universe at all…
You'll be blessed with daughters.

Blessed.

Etymologically "Bless" means: to make bleed.
See? Now it's a lesson in linguistics.
In other words blood speaks.
That's the message.
Stay with me.

Your daughters will teach you
What all men must one day come to know,
That women, made of moonlight, magic, and macabre,
Will make you know the blood.
We'll get it all over the sheets and car seats.

We'll do that.
We introduce you to our insides.

Period.

And if you're as unprepared as we sometimes are,
It'll get all over you and leave a forever stain.

So, to my daughter:

Should any fool mishandle
The wild geography of your body,
How it rides a red running current,
Like any good wolf, or witch, well then...

Just BLEED.

Give that blood a Biblical name,

Something of stone and mortar.
Name it after Eve's first rebellion in that garden.
Name it after the last little girl to have her genitals
Mutilated in Kinshasa (that was this morning),
Give it as many syllables as there are unreported rape cases.

Name the blood something holy.
Something mighty.
Something un-languageable.
Something in hieroglyphs.
Something that sounds like the end of the world.

Name it for the roar between your legs and
For the women who'll not be nameless here.

Just bleed anyhow.

Spill your impossible scripture
All over the good furniture.

Bleed and bleed and bleed

On EVERYTHING he loves...period.

Katrina

the sting and croon of her,
the growl and glint of a storm
that's more than a storm,
the howling wind masquerade
tipping the bayou
into oblivion.

brown-bag boys bobbling
in dirty water on Bourbon Street,
the thunder-smack
of levees breaking
like carnival balloons.

that woman on the roof
can't swim a lick,
her daughter's swollen
in the living room,
her diabetes popped loose,
the insulin's floating
down the street.

diapers, couch,
cushions, and car parts,
all swimming in
the stink of ruptured
sewer lines.

no telling where her daddy is.
the baby went under first,
jaundiced and yelping

no breathable air.

Katrina, the rumbling bitch
who kept hell coming,
the uninitiated rumble
that became a swell,
chewed up the lower 9th Ward,
shook windows from
their frames,
made an awful melody,

bone and wood splintered equally,
caved in supermarkets,
looted and ran through
everybody wading
in the whip of water,
sludge and muck and
the president flying
overhead to see
what floating graves
look like,
the swamp-water fiasco

weeks and weeks before
the Calvary came
with air-dropped
dried goods and bottled water,

when the boys got shot on the bridge,
and the girls were raped in the Super Dome,
after water-filled bodies
filled sidewalks in the French Quarter

like soggy party favors,

the bayou
a terrible Atlantis
peopled by rudderless
men, blistered and drowned,

with no promise
of resurrection.

Carry Your Books With You

You'll need the rhythm of living words
to rage and agonize right.

This is the heavy work,
the get-down-dirty business
of being.
The funk of protests and cities,
the boogaloo rumpus of fire-starters and poets
running down midnight,
and here's the best part:

Your tune will be hip forever.

Hipsters will thumb through your mad history
gleefully, turn it into anthems
for the disenfranchised,
a newer bloodier jazz,

unclassifiable.

And you'll know
writing is resistance,
the peeled back earth
upturned and grinning, saying:

World without end.
Amen.

And your heart?

The impossible beating
of your coliseum heart?

The last American Revolution.

About the Author

Dominique Christina is a mother, an educator and an agitator born and raised in Denver, Colorado 40 years ago. She holds two Masters degrees, in English Literature and Education respectively. A licensed educator, Dominique taught in the Denver and Aurora Public school systems in Colorado for ten years, directed college prep programs and taught in an adjunct capacity at Community College of Aurora and Metropolitan State University of Denver. She believes that words make worlds.

In the slam world (competitive poetry) Dominique began in 2011. That same year she won the National Poetry Slam Championship. In 2012 she won the Women of the World Slam Championship. She won it again in 2014. She's the only person to win that honor twice.

She is a Rocky Mountain Women's Institute fellow. Her work has appeared on TV One's season 3 *Verses and Flow* show. She has performed with Cornel West and was an invited guest to Washington DC to read her poem "Emmett Till" for the Till family and the parents of Trayvon Martin, a young man who was killed in Sanford, Florida.

Her first book of poetry, *The Bones, The Breaking, The Balm*, was published by Penmanship Books 2014. Her second book, a collection of poetry, essays, and writing prompts, is set for publication in October 2015 by Sounds True Publishing.

Her work also appears in numerous literary journals, anthologies, and magazines and has been featured in Huffington Post and Upworthy several times.

Dominique's family was critical in the civil rights movement. Her aunt Carlotta Walls-Lanier was one of nine students to desegregate Central High School in Little Rock, Arkansas. Her grandfather was a shortstop, Hall of Fame baseball player for the Kansas City Monarchs in the Negro Leagues before baseball was integrated. When he left, Jackie Robinson, who would later go on to integrate baseball, took his place. Dominique's mother, Professor Jackie Benton, is named for Jackie Robinson.

She is mother to four wildly expressive children who never use inside voices...ever. But they are the raw material of possible and give her plenty of reasons to praise.

Trigger Warning: Poetry Saved My Life

Compiled and Edited by Zachary Kluckman

$14.95

For decades, the coffee houses, darkly shadowed bar stools, inner city apartments, and subway stations have sounded the echo of this phrase – poetry saved my life. Poets worldwide have uttered these words to one another like a scared truth, a shared secret. Not all of them certainly, but enough. Enough to make this little tome more than a mere collection of voices, but a vital, celebratory reminder that poetry still opens the door for those whose screams are strangled by pillows. Here are the sounds of pleasure heralded against shoulders, the uplifted voices and stark tremolos of those who have survived the turmoil and trembling because they found something so deceptively simple – so heart-wrenchingly real.

Mothers & Daughters A La Palabra: The Word is a Woman Anthology

Compiled and Edited by Jessica Helen Lopez & Katrina K Guarascio
Photography by Mariah Bottomly

$14.95

By way of black and white photography, you will be invited into the home and hearth of women, the familial ties that bind mothers to their daughters and vice versa. It is an intergenerational journey of unconditional love, compassion, faith and sometimes loss, heartbreak and even disappointment. Here are poems and stories of humor, exasperation, healing, and protectiveness. Here are stories about you and yours. La Palabra is a humble collective, a steady heartbeat, a clanging gong.

Observable Acts

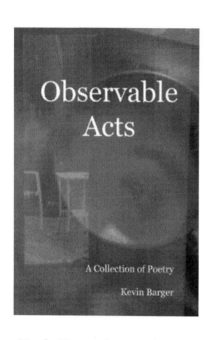

Poetry by Kevin Barger

Cover Art by James Burbank

$10.95

Kevin Barger is a performance poet, writer, and retired slam organizer based in Asheville, NC. He was instrumental in bringing slam poetry back to popularity in Asheville after its rise, fall, and subsequent misfirings in the area by helping to lay the groundwork for Poetry Slam Asheville from 2008 through 2011.
He has also appeared on many other stages in and around the Carolinas including the Lake Eden Arts Festival, Lexington Avenue Arts and Fun Festival, the Individual World Poetry Slam, and Southern Fried in which he was on the first team from Asheville sent to Southern Fried in nearly a decade.
Now, semi-retired from the slam scene but itching to get back on stage again, he has compiled old favorites and new material in *Observable Acts*; his first endeavour onto the published page.

Passion, Provocation, and Prophecy

Interview and Poetry by Jack Hirschman and Justin Desmangles

$10.95

A Pier Paolo Pasolini Dossier

This book is not a collection of Pasolini's work, instead it serves as an ode to him. Beginning with an interview between Jack Hirschman and Justin Desmangles, and followed by two arcanes written by Hirschman which reflect on the man Pasolini was, this slim edition is a companion piece to honor a voice silenced before its time.

I highly recommend adding the book In Danger (City Light Books 2010) as a companion to this book. The book, edited by Jack Hirschman, is a wonderful introduction to Pasolini and his works.

Passion, Provocation and Prophecy is a wonderful dialogue to those who have an interest, love, understanding, and appreciation for not only Pasolini's work but for the man he was.

A Fire of Prayer

Poetry and Photography by Gina Marselle

$15.00

Gina Marselle, M.A.Ed, resides in New Mexico with her husband and children. She is a high school English teacher, and finds enjoyment in being creative through poetry, painting, and photography. She has been awarded three grants for various philanthropy poetic projects. In addition, she has published poetic work with The Sunday Poem Online Series, in the Alibi, the Rag, SIC3, Adobe Walls: An anthology of New Mexico poetry, Catching Calliope, Fix and Free Poetry Anthology I and II, and La Palabra Anthology I and II.

Periscope Heart

Poetry by Kai Coggin

$15.00

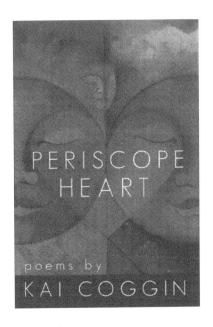

In Coggin's debut collection of poetry, the Heart is the lens through which she leads us in words. Every line is infused with beauty and light and a yearning that is inescapable, palpable. Her voice is precise and piercing, like a song you hum without knowing, because it is already inside you. Her poems carry the fluttering soul, with vivid imagery that is tangible and evocative.

"I first met Kai Coggin as a blazing fire of energy, a supernova educator in the Houston high schools. Now she is on her light path teaching through her own poetry. Her words are spells, chants, prayers, invocations. Thank you, Kai, for work of the spirit, for illuminations like desert thunder and a night sky of benedictions."

- Sandra Cisneros author of House on Mango Street

The Fall of a Sparrow

Poetry
by Katrina K Guarascio

$12.95

Here is a collection of poetic wonderment, musings on the ineffable universal experience of beauty as it is. Real, at times veiled by the uncertain consequence of letting go or giving in, yet always an experience on the lip of the chasm, preparing for wild success or the wailing dismay of failure. Guarascio's poems are filled with beautiful creatures, metaphoric animals crawling amongst the words, haunting the reader with their subtle, but necessary presence.

In these poems are love, loss, resignation, breathlessness, intimacy and touch; the edge of the blade pressing against the plump flesh of the fruit or the slight swell of hipbone under a lover's hand.

Light as a Feather

Compiled and Edited by Katrina K Guarascio

$12.95

"Light as a Feather transports readers into the bleak landscape experienced by so many of us who suffer from eating disorders and depression. We are swept into an exploration of bones clinking "like wind chimes," "blubber like chain mail," "nights so black," and "making friends with bullets." These poems are raw and revealing yet communicate hope through perseverance and love."

Lucretia E. Penny Pence, Associate Professor of Language, Literacy, and Sociocultural Studies

Also available from
Swimming with Elephants Publications. LLC

Some of it is Muscle
Zachary Kluckman

Cunt.Bomb.
Jessica Helen Lopez

September
Katrina K Guarascio & Gina Marselle

Catching Calliope
A Quarterly Poetry Anthology

Verbrennen
Matthew Brown

Loved Always Tomorrow
Emily Bjustrom

Heartbreak Ridge and Other Poems
Bill Nevins

To Anyone Who Has Ever Loved a Writer
Nika Ann

find these titles and many more at:
swimmingwithelephants.com